Faultlines _

MARK WARD

voidspace press _

FAULTLINES _

Copyright © 2024 Mark Ward

voidspace press, 2024

All rights reserved.

ISBN 978-1-739355-20-3

1

We sit across from each other and try
to assign blame. Is the fault YOURS / MINE?

[For YOURS, go to page 2

For MINE, go to page 53]

2

We sit across from each other and try
to assign blame. It's easy. It's YOUR FAULT.

[Go to page 3]

3

We sit across from each other and try
to understand why you did it. Were things
so bad that you had to explode your life?
I'm not sure where to start: THE LIES or HIM.

[For THE LIES, go to page 5

For HIM, go to page 6]

4

We sit across from each other and try
to understand why you did it. Were things
so bad that you had to explode your life?
There's only one place to start – ALL THE LIES.

[Go to page 5]

5

We sit across from each other and try
to understand how you did it. Were things
so bad that you had to explode your life?
You told all your friends that I was dying:
seven months to live, inoperable.
There were STRANGERS WATCHING ME / a GO-FUNDME.

[For STRANGERS WATCHING ME, go to page 7

For a GOFUNDME, go to page 8]

6

I don't want to talk about him.

[Go to page 4]

7

We sit across from each other and try
to understand how you did it. Were things
so bad that you had to explode your life?
You told all your friends that I was dying:
seven months to live, inoperable.
Strange men at a respectful distance,
sighing. Do they APPROACH or MESSAGE ME?

[For APPROACH, go to page 9

For MESSAGE ME, go to page 10]

8

We sit across from each other and try
to understand how you did it. Were things
so bad that you had to explode your life?
You told all your friends that I was dying:
seven months to live, inoperable.
There's a GoFundMe to pay for my next
hospital stay and my operations.
"To Find Out More, click VIDEO or TEXT."

[For VIDEO, go to page 15

For TEXT, go to page 16]

9

We sit across from each other and try
to understand how you did it. Were things
so bad that you had to explode your life?
You told all your friends that I was dying:
seven months to live, inoperable.
Strange men greet me in the supermarket,
ask how I'm doing, sigh, patronise me.
Sometimes they BUY MY SHOPPING / MAKE ME SIT.

[For BUY MY SHOPPING, go to page 11

For MAKE ME SIT, go to page 12]

10

We sit across from each other and try
to understand how you did it. Were things
so bad that you had to explode your life?
You told all your friends that I was dying:
seven months to live, inoperable.
Strange men at a respectful distance,
sighing. At night, they message me, addled,
offering me THEIR LOVE or ASSISTANCE.

[For THEIR LOVE, go to page 13

For ASSISTANCE, go to page 14]

11

We sit across from each other and try
to understand how you did it. Were things
so bad that you had to explode your life?
You told all your friends that I was dying:
seven months to live, inoperable.
Strange men greet me in the supermarket,
ask how I'm doing, sigh, patronise me.
They buy my groceries, carry them out
to my car, say it's shocking I've no help,
ASK WHERE YOU ARE or OFFER TO COME HOME.

[For ASK WHERE YOU ARE, go to page 17

For OFFER TO COME HOME, go to page 18]

12

We sit across from each other and try
to understand how you did it. Were things
so bad that you had to explode your life?
You told all your friends that I was dying:
seven months to live, inoperable.
Strange men greet me in the supermarket,
ask how I'm doing, sigh, patronise me.
Sometimes they push my shoulders, make me sit.
The security guards terrorize me:
"Why did you lie? FOR ATTENTION? MONEY?"

[For ATTENTION, go to page 19

For MONEY, go to page 20]

13

We sit across from each other and try
to understand how you did it. Were things
so bad that you had to explode your life?
You told all your friends that I was dying:
seven months to live, inoperable.
Strange men at a respectful distance,
sighing. At night, they message me, addled,
offering me their love and their dick pics.
One sends me photographs of his whole life.
Pictures of HIM SLEEPING or HIM WORKING.

[For HIM SLEEPING, go to page 21

For HIM WORKING, go to page 22]

14

We sit across from each other and try
to understand how you did it. Were things
so bad that you had to explode your life?
You told all your friends that I was dying:
seven months to live, inoperable.
Strange men at a respectful distance,
sighing. At night, they message me, addled,
they want to offer me some assistance:
to teach me French, mindfulness, common sense.
I choose LOCKPICKING or PRODIGAL SINS.

[For LOCKPICKING, go to page 23

For PRODIGAL SINS, go to page 24]

15

We sit across from each other and try
to understand how you did it. Were things
so bad that you had to explode your life?
You told all your friends that I was dying:
seven months to live, inoperable.
There's a GoFundMe to pay for my next
hospital stay and my operations.
I "Find Out More", click video. I'm left
squinting for movement in an empty frame.
I skip ahead: ONE MINUTE / FIVE MINUTES.

[For ONE MINUTE, go to page 25

For FIVE MINUTES, go to page 26]

16

We sit across from each other and try
to understand how you did it. Were things
so bad that you had to explode your life?
You told all your friends that I was dying:
seven months to live, inoperable.
There's a GoFundMe to pay for my next
hospital stay and my operations.
I "Find Out More" by clicking on the text.
It brings me to an article written
apparently by ME or MY DOCTOR.

[For ME, go to page 27

For MY DOCTOR, go to page 28]

17

We sit across from each other and try
to understand how you did it. Were things
so bad that you had to explode your life?
You told all your friends that I was dying:
seven months to live, inoperable.
Strange men greet me in the supermarket,
ask how I'm doing, sigh, patronise me.
They buy my groceries, carry them out
to my car, say it's shocking I've no help.
"Where is your husband?" And I can't answer.
They come closer and start to whisper "Well
he's been SLEEPING IN THE OFFICE / HIS CAR."

[For SLEEPING IN THE OFFICE, go to page 29

For HIS CAR, go to page 30]

18

We sit across from each other and try
to understand how you did it. Were things
so bad that you had to explode your life?
You told all your friends that I was dying:
seven months to live, inoperable.
Strange men greet me in the supermarket,
ask how I'm doing, sigh, patronise me.
They buy my groceries, carry them out
to my car, say it's shocking I've no help.
One loads the boot and offers to come home.
"I'll follow your car," he says not waiting
for an answer: I DRIVE OFF or I WAIT.

[For I DRIVE OFF, go to page 31

For I WAIT, go to page 32]

19

We sit across from each other and try
to understand how you did it. Were things
so bad that you had to explode your life?
You told all your friends that I was dying:
seven months to live, inoperable.
Strange men greet me in the supermarket,
ask how I'm doing, sigh, patronise me.
Sometimes they push my shoulders, make me sit.
The security guards terrorize me:
"Why did you lie?" He sneers, "For attention?"
The bigger one gets right up in my face,
"I'm watching now." Stares at MY HANDS / MY LIPS.

[For MY HANDS, go to page 33

For MY LIPS, go to page 34]

20

We sit across from each other and try
to understand how you did it. Were things
so bad that you had to explode your life?
You told all your friends that I was dying:
seven months to live, inoperable.
Strange men greet me in the supermarket,
ask how I'm doing, sigh, patronise me.
Sometimes they push my shoulders, make me sit.
The security guards terrorize me:
"Why did you lie?" The smaller one asks "Money?"
but doesn't wait for an answer. "For what?
How much did you want? A LITTLE? A LOT?"

[For A LITTLE, go to page 35

For A LOT, go to page 36]

21

We sit across from each other and try
to understand how you did it. Were things
so bad that you had to explode your life?
You told all your friends that I was dying:
seven months to live, inoperable.
Strange men at a respectful distance,
sighing. At night, they message me, addled,
offering me their love and their dick pics.
One sends me photographs of his whole life.
Pictures of him sleeping, his arm askew,
a pillow embroidered with my likeness.
Caption: "THIS COULD BE YOU" or "THIS IS YOU".

[For THIS COULD BE YOU, go to page 37

For THIS IS YOU, go to page 38]

22

We sit across from each other and try
to understand how you did it. Were things
so bad that you had to explode your life?
You told all your friends that I was dying:
seven months to live, inoperable.
Strange men at a respectful distance,
sighing. At night, they message me, addled,
offering me their love and their dick pics.
One sends me photographs of his whole life.
Pictures of him working at a café,
of him studying, getting a degree,
a new job in FINANCE or MEDICINE.

[For FINANCE, go to page 39

For MEDICINE, go to page 40]

23

We sit across from each other and try
to understand how you did it. Were things
so bad that you had to explode your life?
You told all your friends that I was dying:
seven months to live, inoperable.
Strange men at a respectful distance,
sighing. At night, they message me, addled,
they want to offer me some assistance:
to teach me French, mindfulness, common sense.
I click lockpicking. A large box arrives
far too big for what has been advertised.
I LEAVE IT ON THE PORCH or OPEN IT.

[For LEAVE IT ON THE PORCH, go to page 41

For OPEN IT, go to page 42]

24

We sit across from each other and try
to understand how you did it. Were things
so bad that you had to explode your life?
You told all your friends that I was dying:
seven months to live, inoperable.
Strange men at a respectful distance,
sighing. At night, they message me, addled,
they want to offer me some assistance:
to teach me French, mindfulness, common sense.
I choose Prodigal Sins, a study of
evil in firstborn sons through history.
I READ THE INTRO or LOOK AT THE PICTURES.

[For READ THE INTRO, go to page 43

For LOOK AT THE PICTURES, go to page 44]

25

We sit across from each other and try
to understand how you did it. Were things
so bad that you had to explode your life?
You told all your friends that I was dying:
seven months to live, inoperable.
There's a GoFundMe to pay for my next
hospital stay and my operations.
I "Find Out More", click video. I'm left
squinting for movement in an empty frame.
I skip ahead one minute and see me,
pallid, bald, crying about the cancer.
WHY DON'T I REMEMBER THIS? / WHEN WAS THIS?

[For WHY DON'T I REMEMBER THIS?, go to page 45

For WHEN WAS THIS?, go to page 46]

We sit across from each other and try
to understand how you did it. Were things
so bad that you had to explode your life?
You told all your friends that I was dying:
seven months to live, inoperable.
There's a GoFundMe to pay for my next
hospital stay and my operations.
I "Find Out More", click video. I'm left
squinting for movement in an empty frame.
I skip five minutes and you fill the screen.
You're in the middle of a long story.
You say THAT'S WHAT HAPPENED / THAT'S ALL
OF IT."

[For THAT'S WHAT HAPPENED, go to page 47

For THAT'S ALL OF IT, go to page 48]

27

We sit across from each other and try
to understand how you did it. Were things
so bad that you had to explode your life?
You told all your friends that I was dying:
seven months to live, inoperable.
There's a GoFundMe to pay for my next
hospital stay and my operations.
I "Find Out More" by clicking on the text.
It brings me to an article written
seemingly by me. I describe therein
just how I have been keeping myself alive,
with either fervent PRAYER or FRESH URINE.

[For PRAYER, go to page 49

For FRESH URINE, go to page 50]

We sit across from each other and try
to understand how you did it. Were things
so bad that you had to explode your life?
You told all your friends that I was dying:
seven months to live, inoperable.
There's a GoFundMe to pay for my next
hospital stay and my operations.
I "Find Out More" by clicking on the text.
It brings me to an article written
by my doctor, explaining exactly
my delusion: that you make games, that I'm a poet.
He says this is THERAPY / UNHEALTHY.

[For THERAPY, go to page 51

For UNHEALTHY, go to page 52]

29

We sit across from each other and try
to understand how you did it. Were things
so bad that you had to explode your life?
You told all your friends that I was dying:
seven months to live, inoperable.
Strange men greet me in the supermarket,
ask how I'm doing, sigh, patronise me.
They buy my groceries, carry them out
to my car, say it's shocking I've no help.
"Where is your husband?" And I can't answer.
They come closer and start to whisper that
he's been caught sleeping in his office.
"He looks pale and his work has gone to shit."
They hold my hand, promise to keep me safe.

[Or not. To try again: go to page 1]

30

We sit across from each other and try
to understand how you did it. Were things
so bad that you had to explode your life?
You told all your friends that I was dying:
seven months to live, inoperable.
Strange men greet me in the supermarket,
ask how I'm doing, sigh, patronise me.
They buy my groceries, carry them out
to my car, say it's shocking I've no help.
"Where is your husband?" And I can't answer.
They come closer and start to whisper that
he's been sleeping in his car and washing
in the sink. "Do you not care about him?
Don't you think that you owe him more than this?"

[Or not. To try again: go to page 1]

31

We sit across from each other and try
to understand how you did it. Were things
so bad that you had to explode your life?
You told all your friends that I was dying:
seven months to live, inoperable.
Strange men greet me in the supermarket,
ask how I'm doing, sigh, patronise me.
They buy my groceries, carry them out
to my car, say it's shocking I've no help.
One loads the boot and offers to come home.
"I'll follow your car," he says not waiting
for an answer. I drive home and he's there,
unloading my shopping, his suitcases.
He says he's been looking forward to this.

[Or not. To try again: go to page 1]

32

We sit across from each other and try
to understand how you did it. Were things
so bad that you had to explode your life?
You told all your friends that I was dying:
seven months to live, inoperable.
Strange men greet me in the supermarket,
ask how I'm doing, sigh, patronise me.
They buy my groceries, carry them out
to my car, say it's shocking I've no help.
One loads the boot and offers to come home.
"I'll follow your car," he says not waiting.
I don't move. Two minutes pass. He gets out,
exasperated. "Fine, follow me then."
At his house, I put my food in his fridge.

[Or not. To try again: go to page 1]

33

We sit across from each other and try
to understand how you did it. Were things
so bad that you had to explode your life?
You told all your friends that I was dying:
seven months to live, inoperable.
Strange men greet me in the supermarket,
ask how I'm doing, sigh, patronise me.
Sometimes they push my shoulders, make me sit.
The security guards terrorize me:
"Why did you lie?" He sneers, "For attention?"
The bigger one gets right up in my face,
"I'm watching now." He clasps my hands to him.
"No more lies." The other guard rolls his eyes.
"Tell me everything. START AT THE BEGINNING."

[Go to page 1]

34

We sit across from each other and try
to understand how you did it. Were things
so bad that you had to explode your life?
You told all your friends that I was dying:
seven months to live, inoperable.
Strange men greet me in the supermarket,
ask how I'm doing, sigh, patronise me.
Sometimes they push my shoulders, make me sit.
The security guards terrorize me:
"Why did you lie?" He asks, "For attention?"
The bigger one gets right up in my face,
"I'm watching now." He pulls me to a kiss.
"I see you as you are, like he never
did. He's a fool. I'll kiss you forever."

[Or not. To try again: go to page 1]

35

We sit across from each other and try
to understand how you did it. Were things
so bad that you had to explode your life?
You told all your friends that I was dying:
seven months to live, inoperable.
Strange men greet me in the supermarket,
ask how I'm doing, sigh, patronise me.
Sometimes they push my shoulders, make me sit.
The security guards terrorize me:
"Why did you lie?" The smaller one asks "Money?"
but doesn't wait for an answer. "For what?
How much did you want? I don't have that much,
you can have this." He gives me his wallet.
"I'm happy with my life. I don't need it."

[Or not. To try again: go to page 1]

We sit across from each other and try
to understand how you did it. Were things
so bad that you had to explode your life?
You told all your friends that I was dying:
seven months to live, inoperable.
Strange men greet me in the supermarket,
ask how I'm doing, sigh, patronise me.
Sometimes they push my shoulders, make me sit.
The security guards terrorize me:
"Why did you lie?" The smaller one asks "Money?"
but doesn't wait for an answer. "For what?
How much did you want? You wanted a lot,
right? To start a new life? To disappear."
He opens his coat. "You can hide in here."

[Or not. To try again: go to page 1]

37

We sit across from each other and try
to understand how you did it. Were things
so bad that you had to explode your life?
You told all your friends that I was dying:
seven months to live, inoperable.
Strange men at a respectful distance,
sighing. At night, they message me, addled,
offering me their love and their dick pics.
One sends me photographs of his whole life.
Pictures of him sleeping, his arm askew,
a pillow embroidered with my likeness.
"If you were brave enough, this could be you."
I scoff, but in the corner of the pic,
you're there, laughing, wide-eyed, at your own shtick.

[Or not. To try again: go to page 1]

38

We sit across from each other and try
to understand how you did it. Were things
so bad that you had to explode your life?
You told all your friends that I was dying:
seven months to live, inoperable.
Strange men at a respectful distance,
sighing. At night, they message me, addled,
offering me their love and their dick pics.
One sends me photographs of his whole life.
Pictures of him sleeping, his arm around
a pillow embroidered with my likeness.
The aggressively lowercase caption
insists "this is you". I'm here on my bed
but I can feel him fold me. All is dark.

[Or not. To try again: go to page 1]

39

We sit across from each other and try
to understand how you did it. Were things
so bad that you had to explode your life?
You told all your friends that I was dying:
seven months to live, inoperable.
Strange men at a respectful distance,
sighing. At night, they message me, addled,
offering me their love and their dick pics.
One sends me photographs of his whole life.
Pictures of him working at a café,
of him studying, getting a degree,
starting a new job in finance. "Are you proud
of me?" he asks. I don't reply. "Can't you
see how hard I've worked? Check your bank account."

[Or not. To try again: go to page 1]

40

We sit across from each other and try
to understand how you did it. Were things
so bad that you had to explode your life?
You told all your friends that I was dying:
seven months to live, inoperable.
Strange men at a respectful distance,
sighing. At night, they message me, addled,
offering me their love and their dick pics.
One sends me photographs of his whole life.
Pictures of him working at a café,
of him studying, getting a degree,
becoming a doctor. "It's all for you,"
he tells me. "I want to keep you healthy,
to be with you as long as I can be."

[Or not. To try again: go to page 1]

41

We sit across from each other and try
to understand how you did it. Were things
so bad that you had to explode your life?
You told all your friends that I was dying:
seven months to live, inoperable.
Strange men at a respectful distance,
sighing. At night, they message me, addled,
they want to offer me some assistance:
to teach me French, mindfulness, common sense.
I click lockpicking. A large box arrives
far too big for what has been advertised.
I leave it on the porch but hear it cry.
A man's voice says "I just wanted to know where
you live. We can learn together. Let's try."

[Or not. To try again: go to page 1]

42

We sit across from each other and try
to understand how you did it. Were things
so bad that you had to explode your life?
You told all your friends that I was dying:
seven months to live, inoperable.
Strange men at a respectful distance,
sighing. At night, they message me, addled,
they want to offer me some assistance:
to teach me French, mindfulness, common sense.
I click lockpicking. A large box arrives
far too big for what has been advertised.
I open it and find pictures of you,
expertly collaged and framed to convey
exactly where you've been and why you left.

[Or not. To try again: go to page 1]

43

We sit across from each other and try
to understand how you did it. Were things
so bad that you had to explode your life?
You told all your friends that I was dying:
seven months to live, inoperable.
Strange men at a respectful distance,
sighing. At night, they message me, addled,
they want to offer me some assistance:
to teach me French, mindfulness, common sense.
I pick Prodigal Sins, a study of
evil in firstborn sons through history.
I read the introduction. I'm mentioned
fourteen times; always in comparison
to evil men who you say I'm worse than.

[Or not. To try again: go to page 1]

44

We sit across from each other and try
to understand how you did it. Were things
so bad that you had to explode your life?
You told all your friends that I was dying:
seven months to live, inoperable.
Strange men at a respectful distance,
sighing. At night, they message me, addled,
they want to offer me some assistance:
to teach me French, mindfulness, common sense.
I pick Prodigal Sins, a study of
evil in firstborn sons through history.
I look at the pictures and see myself
bald in photoshopped fundraising posters
that you made. The book says I'm revolting.

[Or not. To try again: go to page 1]

45

We sit across from each other and try
to understand how you did it. Were things
so bad that you had to explode your life?
You told all your friends that I was dying:
seven months to live, inoperable.
There's a GoFundMe to pay for my next
hospital stay and my operations.
I "Find Out More", click video. I'm left
squinting for movement in an empty frame.
I skip ahead one minute and see me,
crying about the cancer, how I thought
I could beat it. I don't remember this.
And you explain that it's a side-effect.
You hold my hand, say "You always forget".

[Or not. To try again: go to page 1]

We sit across from each other and try
to understand how you did it. Were things
so bad that you had to explode your life?
You told all your friends that I was dying:
seven months to live, inoperable.
There's a GoFundMe to pay for my next
hospital stay and my operations.
I "Find Out More", click video. I'm left
squinting for movement in an empty frame.
I skip ahead one minute and see me,
pallid, bald, crying about the cancer
I had tried so hard to beat. When was this?
The timestamp says 2014. Six years.
Where did you go? What happened? How am I here?

[Or not. To try again: go to page 1]

47

We sit across from each other and try
to understand how you did it. Were things
so bad that you had to explode your life?
You told all your friends that I was dying:
seven months to live, inoperable.
There's a GoFundMe to pay for my next
hospital stay and my operations.
I "Find Out More", click video. I'm left
squinting for movement in an empty frame.
I skip five minutes and you fill the screen.
You're in the middle of a long story
about something I said I didn't mean.
You say that's what happened but don't explain
how I died. I touch the screen, start to fade.

[Or not. To try again: go to page 1]

48

We sit across from each other and try
to understand how you did it. Were things
so bad that you had to explode your life?
You told all your friends that I was dying:
seven months to live, inoperable.
There's a GoFundMe to pay for my next
hospital stay and my operations.
I "Find Out More", click video. I'm left
squinting for movement in an empty frame.
I skip five minutes and you fill the screen.
You're in the middle of a long story.
about how easy it was to con you:
a stock image boyfriend, a younger me
photoshopped into your begging letters.

[Or not. To try again: go to page 1]

49

We sit across from each other and try
to understand how you did it. Were things
so bad that you had to explode your life?
You told all your friends that I was dying:
seven months to live, inoperable.
There's a GoFundMe to pay for my next
hospital stay and my operations.
I "Find Out More" by clicking on the text.
It brings me to an article written
seemingly by me. I describe therein
just how I have been keeping myself alive,
mostly with prayers, well, they're invocations.
I ask the universe to please oblige.
Your lifeforce flows into me; I watch you die.

[Or not. To try again: go to page 1]

50

We sit across from each other and try
to understand how you did it. Were things
so bad that you had to explode your life?
You told all your friends that I was dying:
seven months to live, inoperable.
There's a GoFundMe to pay for my next
hospital stay and my operations.
I "Find Out More" by clicking on the text.
It brings me to an article written
seemingly by me. I describe therein
just how I have been keeping myself alive,
mostly with fresh urine. That's what I'll say.
Tied up, you beg me to take your kidney.
I say thank you and unsheathe my new knife.

[Or not. To try again: go to page 1]

51

We sit across from each other and try
to understand how you did it. Were things
so bad that you had to explode your life?
You told all your friends that I was dying:
seven months to live, inoperable.
There's a GoFundMe to pay for my next
hospital stay and my operations.
I "Find Out More" by clicking on the text.
It brings me to an article written
by my doctor, explaining exactly
my delusion: that you make games, that I'm a poet
that it can be therapeutic to dream
but it's not real. You ask the day, the time.
I don't know. The code is gone so I lie.

[Or not. To try again: go to page 1]

52

We sit across from each other and try
to understand how you did it. Were things
so bad that you had to explode your life?
You told all your friends that I was dying:
seven months to live, inoperable.
There's a GoFundMe to pay for my next
hospital stay and my operations.
I "Find Out More" by clicking on the text.
It brings me to an article written
by my doctor, explaining exactly
my delusion: that you make games, that I'm a poet.
He says this is unhealthy and critiques
my woolly metre, abandoned rhyme scheme,
my code, which if you were real, you'd laugh at.

[Or not. To try again: go to page 1]

53

I'm not the one at fault here.

YOU'RE RIGHT. / YOU ARE.

[For YOU'RE RIGHT, go to page 2

For YOU ARE, go to page 54]

54

It really hurts me that you'd think that. I don't think that's very helpful.

I'M NOT TRYING TO HURT YOU. / IT'S ALL YOUR FAULT.

[For I'M NOT TRYING TO HURT YOU, go to page 55

For IT'S ALL YOUR FAULT, go to page 56]

Good.

[Go to page 2]

Here we go, this again. I'm to blame for everything, right?

Right?

TO BE HONEST, YOU KIND OF ARE. / THAT'S NOT REALLY WHAT I MEANT.

[For TO BE HONEST, YOU KIND OF ARE, go to page 57

For THAT'S NOT REALLY WHAT I MEANT, go to page 58]

You're spiteful, you know that. This is why I'm not with you anymore.

That's not true.

Well, what then.

It's because of YOUR JEALOUSY. / YOUR INSECURITIES. / YOUR INABILITY TO BE FUCKING HAPPY.

[For YOUR JEALOUSY, go to page 59

For YOUR INSECURITIES, go to page 59

For YOUR INABILITY TO BE FUCKING HAPPY, go to page 59]

If you're going to trip over your words, we should just start over.

[Go to page 2]

You don't get to offer options. What do you think this is? This is my world we're in.

Now, are you going to behave?

YES. / NO.

[For YES, go to page 60

For NO, go to page 61]

60

Promise?

YES

[Go to page 62]

I said, are you going to behave?

YES

[Go to page 62]

IT'S ALL[1] YOUR FAULT[2]
IT'S ALL[3] YOUR FAULT[4]
IT'S ALL[5] YOUR FAULT[6]
IT'S ALL[7] YOUR FAULT[8]
IT'S ALL[9] YOUR FAULT[10]
IT'S ALL[11] YOUR FAULT[12]
IT'S ALL[13] YOUR FAULT[14]
IT'S ALL[15] YOUR FAULT[16]
IT'S ALL[17] YOUR FAULT[18]
IT'S ALL[19] YOUR FAULT[20]
IT'S ALL[21] YOUR FAULT[22]
IT'S ALL[23] YOUR FAULT[24]
IT'S ALL[25] YOUR FAULT[26]
IT'S ALL[27] YOUR FAULT[28]

[Go to Endnotes, page 67, and find the relevant footnote]

~~TURN AHEAD~~

-

~~[Go to page 62]~~

~~TURN UP~~

-

~~[Go to page 62]~~

~~WRONG TURN~~
-

~~[Go to page 62]~~

Faultlines

You aren't sitting across from me at all.
I haven't seen you in at least five years.
We didn't love each other anymore.
We had become an inconvenience.
You told me there was someone else you liked.
You hadn't cheated. That's not who you were.
I was barely in the relationship.
Our callousness broke something inside me.

I told you, you should go and be happy.
I moved on with my life. We didn't talk.
I didn't play your game. I wrote some poems.
I learned to code. Fractal breakups. Obsessed.
I got worse. I knew this poem was coming.
The truth. How unattainable that is.

Endnotes

[1.] Go to page 44
[2.] Go to page 29
[3.] Go to page 46
[4.] Go to page 40
[5.] Go to page 32
[6.] Go to page 38
[7.] Go to page 30
[8.] Go to page 49
[9.] Go to page 45
[10.] Go to page 51
[11.] Go to page 37
[12.] Go to page 31
[13.] Go to page 34
[14.] Go to page 36
[15.] Go to page 63
[16.] Go to page 66
[17.] Go to page 65
[18.] Go to page 64

19. Go to page 43
20. Go to page 42
21. Go to page 35
22. Go to page 52
23. Go to page 33
24. Go to page 39
25. Go to page 48
26. Go to page 50
27. Go to page 47
28. Go to page 41

About the Author

Mark Ward is [...click to read more]

www.ingramcontent.com/pod-product-compliance
Lightning Source LLC
Chambersburg PA
CBHW052205070526
44585CB00017B/2080